frolic
Preschool Bible

By Lucy Bell   **Illustrated by Natasha Rimmington**

SPARK
HOUSE
FAMILY
sparkhousefamily.org

OLD TESTAMENT STORIES

NEW TESTAMENT STORIES

WELCOME TO THE FROLIC PRESCHOOL BIBLE!

Look inside these pages to find 40 Bible stories written especially for preschoolers. As you enjoy these stories together, try these tips to build your child's reading skills and biblical literacy.

READING LITERACY TIPS

- Help develop a love of reading by planning cozy, unhurried reading time together.
- When you reread stories, ask what your child remembers about the story from the last time.
- Ask your child to point to words they can recognize.
- See if your child can use picture cues to figure out what's happening in each story.

BIBLICAL LITERACY TIPS

- Point out that the charming Frolic animal characters introduce stories in two parts of the Bible—the Old Testament and New Testament.
- Make connections between Bible stories and things in your child's world, like animals, bodies of water, and foods they recognize.
- At the end of each story, read the simple takeaway to help your child make connections between the story and their faith community.

When you read these Bible stories together, you are building a foundation of faith and a love of God's Word that can last a lifetime!

OLD TESTAMENT STORIES

Creation

In the beginning, there was nothing—except for God.

Then God breathed and began to speak.

"Light! Let there be light!" God made light. And it was good.

"Sky! Let there be sky!" God made the sky. And it was good.

"Water and land! Plants and trees! Sun, moon, stars!" God made them all. And it was good.

"Fish and birds and wild animals!"
God made living creatures. And it was good.

"People! Let there be people!"
God saw all of creation, and it was very good.

Then God rested.

We are part of God's good creation.

Noah

"Noah! Build a boat," God said. "Fill it with animals."

Two at a time, animals crawled, flew, and waddled onto the boat.

Noah and his family hurried inside. A storm began!

For 40 days, rain poured from the sky.

A flood covered the whole world with water.

8

Finally the rain stopped. The water dried up.

Two at a time, animals slithered, hopped, and wriggled off the boat.

Noah and his family hurried outside. The flood was over!

God put a rainbow in the sky.

"I will never flood the earth again," God promised.

God keeps promises to us.

Abraham and Sarah

"Abraham! I will bless you," God said. "You will have a family too big to count—more family than stars in the sky!"

"How can this be?" thought Abraham. "My wife Sarah and I have no children." But he believed God's promise.

When Abraham told Sarah, she laughed and laughed. "I am so old! How can I have a baby?" she wondered.

God's promise was true!

God blessed Abraham and Sarah with a baby named Isaac.

And their family kept growing. It became too big to count. They had more people in their family than stars in the sky!

You are a blessing from God to your family.

Jacob and Esau

Isaac grew up and married Rebekah. They had two sons—twins!

But these brothers were very different.

Esau was born first. He was hairy and strong and hunted outside.

Jacob was born second. He had smooth skin and was quiet and stayed inside.

As Isaac grew old, he got ready to bless Esau, his oldest son.

But Jacob wanted his father's blessing! He planned a trick.

He knew his father could not see well. He put fur on his arms so he would feel like hairy Esau.

Isaac touched his son's arms and blessed Jacob.

All of God's children are blessed.

Joseph and His Brothers

Jacob had 12 sons. But he had only one colorful robe. He gave it to Joseph.

Joseph showed off his father's gift. His older brothers grumbled.

They felt angry and jealous. They didn't want Joseph around. They found a way to get rid of him.
But God was with Joseph and kept him safe.

Many years later, the brothers did not have enough to eat.

They traveled far away to find food. They didn't recognize the man who had food to share.

"It's me!" Joseph told his brothers. "I forgive you for being angry. I want to help you."

Families say "I forgive you" to each other.

Baby Moses

Baby Moses was in danger! His mother wanted to keep him safe.
She put Moses in a basket to hide him in the Nile River.
Moses was safe and dry.

Moses' sister Miriam followed the basket
as it floated down the river.

"Who will feed and care for Moses?"
she wondered.

A princess found the basket! She picked up Baby Moses and held him in her arms.

Miriam had an idea. She told the princess, "My mother and I can help feed and care for this baby."

Baby Moses was safe!

Families keep each other safe.

The Burning Bush

Moses saw a bush on fire, but it did not burn up!
"What is happening?" wondered Moses.

"Moses!" called a voice from the bush. "My people need help." The voice was God's voice!

God told Moses to go to Egypt and talk to Pharaoh. Pharaoh was hurting God's people.

Moses listened to God and went to Egypt. He felt afraid, but God helped Moses be brave.

Moses told Pharaoh, "You are hurting God's people. God says, 'Let my people go!'"

Pharaoh told Moses, "No! No! No! I will not let God's people go!"

God helps us be brave.

The Red Sea

Pharaoh would not listen to Moses, so bad things began to happen to Pharaoh's people.

Frogs hopped and plopped all over. Flies buzzed and bit!

Animals became sick, and the people got itchy, sore skin. The sky was dark all day and all night.

Finally Pharaoh told Moses, "Yes, yes, yes. I will let God's people go."

Moses led God's people to the Red Sea. But Pharaoh changed his mind. He told his soldiers to chase them. They were trapped!

Moses raised his arm. God pushed the water back. The people walked on dry land to the other side.

They sang and danced and thanked God.

We can thank God for helping us.

Manna in the Desert

The people complained to Moses.
"We're hungry! We're hot! We want to go back!"

"God, do you hear your people?" asked Moses.
"We need your help."

God heard the hungry people.

God gave them a kind of bread called manna. Each morning, flakes of manna fell from the sky. The people picked up the food and ate. God gave enough for everyone to eat each day.

God gives us what we need each day.

The Ten Commandments

Moses climbed a mountain to listen to God. God spoke to him!

When Moses climbed back down, he was carrying two stones. Each one had rules written on it.

"God loves us. God gave us these Ten Commandments," Moses told the people. "These will teach us how to love God and each other."

The people listened to Moses. "We can learn God's Ten Commandments," they said. "We can do our best to follow God's teachings."

We follow God's Ten Commandments.

Joshua at Jericho

"Joshua!" God called. "You are now the leader of my people. I will be with you wherever you go." So Joshua led the people to Jericho.

Joshua and all the people looked up. Tall walls! They looked left. Big walls! They looked right. Wide walls! "How will we get into Jericho, God?" Joshua asked.

"March around the city. Blow seven horns," God told Joshua. So God's people marched. Stomp, stomp, stomp! They blew the horns. Toot, toot, toot!

"Make lots of noise! Shout, clap, yell!" God commanded.
God's people shouted, clapped, and yelled.

Crack! Boom! Crash! The walls of Jericho tumbled down.
God's people hurried into the city.

God is with us wherever we go.

Deborah

Deborah was a judge, a listener, and a helper. God chose Deborah to lead the people.

Whenever they needed help, God's people asked wise Deborah.

Stuck? Ask Deborah. Angry? Ask Deborah. Worried? Ask Deborah.

Where's Deborah? Sitting under her palm tree!

When God's people were in danger from enemies, Deborah knew what to do. She called a soldier named Barak.

"Help God's people," she said.

"I'm scared," said Barak. "I'm not going unless you go too."

"I'll go with you," Deborah told him, "and God will help us!"

Barak and Deborah led their soldiers against the enemy army. They won!

God sends wise people to lead us.

Naomi and Ruth

Naomi and Ruth had hungry stomachs, but no food. There was no grain to make bread.

Naomi frowned. "Go back to your family," Naomi told Ruth. "They'll give you food."

Ruth hugged Naomi. "You're my family now," Ruth said. "Your God is my God. I'll stay with you." Naomi smiled. Ruth smiled too.

Ruth saw a field with plenty of grain. A farmer named Boaz called to Ruth. "You can collect leftover grain from my field," Boaz said. "Take as much as you need."

"Thank you, Boaz," Ruth said. She gathered pieces of grain. Ruth and Naomi used it to make bread. No more hungry stomachs!

God gives us family to care for us.

Hannah and Samuel

"I love you, Samuel!" Hannah smiled at her baby. Samuel giggled and cooed.

Hannah thanked God for her baby. She promised to teach Samuel to serve God as he grew.

One night, Samuel woke up suddenly.

"Samuel!" a voice called. He didn't know that voice. Who was calling his name? Samuel went back to sleep.

"Samuel!" Samuel woke up again. Did someone need help outside? Who was calling his name?

"Samuel!" Samuel heard his name again! This time he knew. It must be God's voice!

"Speak to me, God! I am listening," Samuel said.

Families teach children to serve God.

David and Goliath

Big Goliath! Tall Goliath! Giant Goliath! "Send a man to fight me!" Goliath shouted.

The king was afraid. His men were afraid. Everyone was afraid, except David!

David wanted to fight Goliath. "You're just a child! A shepherd!" shouted the king and his men.

"I can do it!" David told them. "God is with me!"

David pulled out his slingshot. He picked up a smooth stone.

"You can't fight me!" laughed Goliath. "You're just a child! A shepherd!"

"I can do it!" David told him. "God is with me!"

Brave David threw the stone. It whistled through the air. Thunk! It hit Goliath right in the forehead! Goliath fell. David won!

God is with us so we can do brave things.

Queen Esther

King Xerxes ruled the land. Queen Esther was his wife. But he did not know Queen Esther was one of God's people.

Haman was a leader in the king's court. He wanted to hurt all of God's people!

Queen Esther learned about Haman's plan. She was worried. "I want the king to protect my people," she thought, "but what if he says no?"

Queen Esther stood before the king. "I am one of God's people. Will you please protect them?" Queen Esther asked him.

King Xerxes said, "Yes!" They were safe!

"Hooray for brave Queen Esther!" God's people cheered.

God helps us stand up for what's right.

The Lord Is My Shepherd

David wrote many songs praising God.
In one, he said God is like a shepherd.

Every day a shepherd cares for his sheep.

He gives them everything they need.

He brings them to green grass.

He finds cool water for them to drink.

He leads them down a safe path.

The shepherd protects his sheep from danger.
He uses his staff to keep them close by.
"Don't be afraid. I will keep you safe," the shepherd tells his sheep.
God loves us like the shepherd loves his sheep.

God is like a loving shepherd to us.

The Fiery Furnace

"Bow down to this statue!" ordered the king.

"We will not bow down!" three men said.
"Not to the tallest statue. Not to a golden statue.
We worship only God. The king is not God."

The king was angry! He wanted to hurt them.

He put the three men in a furnace. It was very hot!

"1...2...3...4?" counted the king. "Who is the fourth man in the furnace?" he asked.

It was an angel of God who protected the three men from the heat.

The king was amazed! "They worship only God," said the king. "I will worship God too."

God protects us in surprising ways.

Daniel

"Pray to the king," the king's law said, "or be thrown to the lions!" But Daniel prayed only to God.

The king's men heard Daniel praying. "To the lions!" they shouted. Daniel tumbled down into the lions' den. Lion eyes blinked. Lion tongues slurped. Lion voices rumbled.

"Dear God," Daniel prayed, "have mercy on me."

The sun went down that evening. The sun came up the next morning. The king and his men peeked into the lions' den. Daniel was safe! God's angel had closed the lions' mouths. They couldn't even roar!

The king was amazed. He cheered, "God has saved him!"

God hears our prayers.

Jonah

"Jonah!" God called. "Go to Nineveh and share my message."

But Jonah didn't want to go. He tried to hide from God by going on a boat.

Soon a storm began to rock it back and forth.

"Get off this boat!" the sailors shouted at Jonah. They threw him into the sea!

Splash! Slurp! Gulp! A giant fish swallowed Jonah.

The fish's belly was dark and stinky and lonely.

"Dear God," Jonah prayed, "I'm sorry I didn't go to Nineveh. I'm sorry I tried to hide. Please give me another chance."

Rumble! Blurp! Splat! The fish spit Jonah out onto the beach. Jonah hurried to Nineveh to share God's message.

God always gives us another chance.

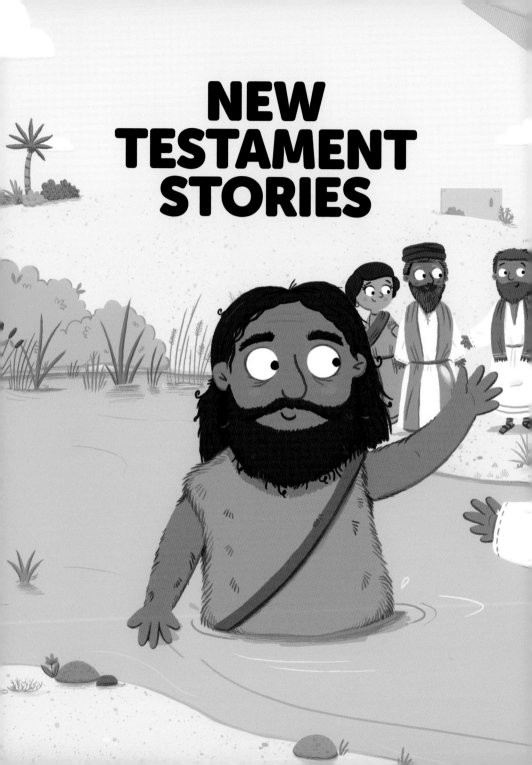

NEW
TESTAMENT
STORIES

An Angel Visits

"Greetings, Mary!" called the angel Gabriel. "The Lord is with you!"
The sparkling stranger surprised her. "Who is this?" Mary wondered.

"Don't be afraid," Gabriel said. "God sent me to bring you good news.
You are going to have a baby named Jesus. He will be God's Son."

"How is this possible?" Mary asked Gabriel.

Gabriel said, "Nothing is impossible with God!"

Mary said, "I love God. I will serve God. I will get ready for Baby Jesus."

God can do what seems impossible.

Jesus Is Born

"The baby is coming soon!" Mary told Joseph.

Joseph was worried. They were traveling away from home.

The town of Bethlehem was still far away.

Where would Jesus be born? Would anyone have room for them?

Mary and Joseph found a stable where they could stay. Baby Jesus was born! They laid him in a manger.

In a field nearby, an angel appeared to some shepherds and said, "A Savior is born!" Then angels filled the sky and sang, "Glory to God! Peace on earth!"

The shepherds hurried to visit the new baby.

We celebrate Baby Jesus at Christmas!

Wise Men

"Look!" one wise man called to the others. "A bright new star is shining in the sky." They all looked up at the star.

"A child has been born who is a king!" another wise man said. "Let's find him."

The wise men began their journey to find Jesus, the new king. Night after night, they followed the star to Bethlehem.

"Look!" one wise man called to the others. "We found him!"

The wise men saw young Jesus. They bowed low. Then they gave three gifts to him—sparkling gold, sweet frankincense, and spicy myrrh. Their gifts honored Jesus, God's Son.

Jesus is a gift to us.

Young Jesus in the Temple

"Jesus!" Mary called out. "Where are you, Jesus?"

His family was very worried. Jesus had been with them when they came to Jerusalem. Now it was time to walk home, but they couldn't find him.

Joseph frowned. "Keep looking. He must be somewhere." They searched for three days!

"Jesus!" Mary called out. "There you are!"

Jesus was in the temple, talking to the teachers. They were amazed at how much Jesus knew. He was only 12 years old!

"Why were you searching for me?" Jesus asked. "Didn't you know I was in my Father's house?"

Then Jesus returned home with his family. He kept growing and learning.

God sends teachers to help us grow and learn.

Jesus Is Baptized

John stood in the Jordan River. "Get ready! Prepare for Jesus!" he called.

He baptized people by dipping them in the water. He told them about God's forgiveness.

One day Jesus waded into the river with John. "Baptize me," he said to John. So John dipped Jesus into the river.

A dove flew down from the sky. God's voice rang out. "This is my beloved Son," God said. "I am pleased with him."

We are all God's beloved children.

Jesus Calls Disciples

Jesus saw some fishermen by the Sea of Galilee. He called them to be his disciples.

"Peter and Andrew! James and John!" Jesus called. "Drop your nets and follow me!"

Women and men! Girls and boys!
Jesus called all kinds of people to share his good news.
Many said, "Yes!"
They followed Jesus. They learned from Jesus. They loved Jesus.

We are disciples of Jesus too.

The Good Samaritan

Jesus told a story about
being a good neighbor.

"Wait! I'm hurt!" a man said to a priest walking by.

But the priest turned away. He did not help the man.

"Stop!" the man yelled. "I need help!"

Another traveler saw the hurt man. He passed right by him.

No one acted like a neighbor. No one cared or helped.

A kind man from Samaria stopped.

"You need a place to rest and heal," he said.
He put bandages on the hurt man.

"I will give you a ride and find help for you." And he did.

The Samaritan man was a good neighbor. He cared and he helped.

Jesus wants us to be good neighbors too.

Jesus Blesses Children

Jumping and clapping. Wriggling and giggling. Smiling and laughing. The children were excited to meet Jesus!

But the disciples said, "No! Don't bother us. Jesus is for grown-ups, not for children."

The children frowned. Their parents sighed. They turned to go home.

"Wait!" called Jesus. "Let the children come to me. The kingdom of God belongs to them."

Running and hopping. Toddling and crawling. Skipping and walking. The children hurried to meet Jesus!

Jesus reached out to them. He held them and blessed each one.

Jesus loves and blesses each child.

Mary and Martha

Two sisters heard the news—Jesus was coming to their house!

"We need to get ready for our friend!" Martha told Mary.

Martha wanted the best for Jesus. The cleanest floor. The most delicious food. Martha hurried to cook and clean.

Jesus arrived at their home with some disciples. Martha called to her sister, "Mary, come help me!"

But Mary wasn't hurrying. She was sitting. Sitting with Jesus! Sitting with the disciples!

"Jesus," Martha said, "tell my sister to help me."

"Martha, don't worry about those things," Jesus told her. "Your sister has chosen what is most important."

Paying attention to Jesus is the most important thing for us.

The Lost Sheep and Coin

Jesus told a story about two people who looked for what they had lost.

"Oh no!" a shepherd cried. "One of my sheep is missing!" He looked by the bush. No sheep! He looked on the hill. No sheep! He looked and looked until...hooray! The lost sheep was found.

God is like the shepherd who found his sheep.

"1...2...3..." a woman counted her coins, but one was missing! She looked on the table. No coin! She looked behind the basket. No coin! She looked and looked until...hooray! The lost coin was found.

God is like the woman who found her coin.

God always knows where to find us.

The Prodigal Son

Jesus told a story about a man with two sons.

"Father!" said the younger son. "I want my share of your money. Now!"

His father gave it to him. The younger son left.

Far from home, he spent all the money. New clothes! Tasty food! Fun parties!

Soon he had nothing left. He was hungry and had to stay with the pigs.

He decided to return home.

His father rushed to meet him. "You're back!" he rejoiced.

The father celebrated his son's return. New clothes!
Tasty food! A fun party!

"Why are you happy?" the older son asked.
"He left. I stayed and helped!"

"I thought your brother was gone forever!"
the father said. "I'm glad he's home!"

God always welcomes us home.

Jesus Teaches and Heals

Jesus was a teacher.

He taught people about God's love.

He told stories about the kingdom of God.

He talked about caring for each other and caring for God's world.

Jesus wanted people to learn as much as they could about God.

Jesus was a healer.

He cared for people who were sick.

He helped people walk again.
He helped blind people see.

He touched people with sores.
The sores went away!

Jesus loved people. He healed them and sent them home.

The people believed. They told everyone what Jesus did!

Jesus still teaches and heals us.

Man Through a Roof

"How will we get in? There's no room to see Jesus!" a man said.
Four men wanted Jesus to help their friend walk again.

But the house was full of people listening to Jesus teach about God.
"We can't get through the door," said one friend.
"Or the window," said another. "Let's bring our friend up to the roof!"

So the four friends dug a hole through the roof!
Jesus looked up. The men lowered down their friend.
"I am God's Son," Jesus said to him. "Get up and walk."
The man stood up! Everyone in the house saw Jesus' miracle.

Jesus' miracles teach us about healing.

Woman at the Well

The sun was hot and Jesus was tired! He sat down at the edge of a well.

A woman from Samaria walked up carrying her water jar.

"Would you give me a drink?" Jesus asked the Samaritan woman.

Then he said something that surprised her.

"I can give you living water," Jesus told her. "Living water will fill you up with God's love! You will never be thirsty again."

"This man must be God's Son," the Samaritan woman realized. She ran to share the good news about Jesus with others.

Jesus gives us living water.

Jesus Feeds a Crowd

A big crowd of people gathered to hear Jesus teach.
They were very hungry, but there wasn't any food for them!

"What will we do?" one disciple asked Jesus.

"I can share my lunch," said a boy. "I have five loaves of bread
and two fish!"

"That's not enough for all these people!" another disciple said.

Jesus smiled at the boy and held the food.
He blessed the five loaves of bread and two fish.
Then the disciples began to pass out the boy's lunch.
There was enough for everyone—even leftovers!
Everyone in the crowd saw Jesus' miracle.

Jesus' miracles teach us about sharing.

Jesus, the Good Shepherd

Jesus told his followers about a good shepherd and his sheep.

A good shepherd calls his sheep by name.
A good shepherd leads his sheep to safety.
A good shepherd knows his sheep, and they know him.
He loves his sheep, and his sheep love him.

Jesus says to us, "I know you by name."

Jesus says to us, "I will lead you so you are safe."

Jesus says to us, "I know my sheep, and my sheep know me."

"I am the Good Shepherd," Jesus tells us. "You are my sheep."

Jesus is our Good Shepherd.

Jesus Dies

The food was ready. The table was ready.

Jesus and his disciples were ready to eat. Jesus knew this would be their last supper together.

"Eat this bread. Drink from this cup," Jesus told them. "Do this to remember me."

After the meal, soldiers took Jesus away from his friends. They brought him to their leaders.

The leaders did not believe Jesus was God's Son. They wanted to hurt him. They ordered the soldiers to nail Jesus to a cross.

Jesus prayed to God, "Father, forgive them."

Then Jesus died on the cross.

We remember that Jesus died on the cross.

Jesus Rises

After Jesus died on the cross, his friends put his body in a tomb.

They covered the opening with a huge stone.

On Sunday morning, some women walked to the tomb. They wanted to take care of Jesus' body.

The stone had been rolled away. Jesus' body was not there—the tomb was empty!

The women saw a man standing in the garden. It was Jesus!

"Jesus!" they shouted. "You are alive!"

"Go find my disciples," Jesus said. "Tell them the good news."

The women ran and cheered, "We have seen the Lord! Jesus is risen! He is alive!"

Tell others that Jesus is alive!

Go and Tell

Jesus died on a cross. On the third day, he rose from the dead!

When he saw his disciples, he said, "Do not be afraid. Peace be with you."

Then Jesus told them to meet him on a mountain in Galilee.

On the mountain, Jesus told them he had God's power on earth and in heaven.

"When I was with you, you followed me and learned from me," he said. "Now it is your turn! Go and tell others about me. Share God's love everywhere."
Jesus promised he would always be with them.

Jesus is always with us.

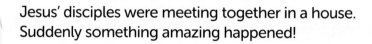

The Holy Spirit

Jesus' disciples were meeting together in a house.
Suddenly something amazing happened!

Whoosh! Swoosh! A loud rushing sound filled the air.

Crackle! Hiss! A fiery flame burned above each
disciple.

The wind and the fire filled them with the Holy Spirit.

Then something even more amazing happened! The disciples began to talk to people from many lands. They could speak in different languages! Everyone could understand what they were saying about Jesus.

The gift of the Holy Spirit made all these amazing things happen.

The Holy Spirit helps us share Jesus with people.

frolic
Preschool Bible

First edition published 2017

Printed in USA

23 22 21 20 19 18   2 3 4 5 6 7 8

ISBN: 9781506420776

Written by Lucy Bell
Illustrated by Natasha Rimmington
Designed by Tim Palin Creative

Library of Congress Cataloging-in-Publication Data

Names: Bell, Lucy J., author. | Rimmington, Natasha, illustrator.
Title: Frolic preschool Bible / by Lucy Bell ; illustrated by Natasha Rimmington.
Description: First edition. | Minneapolis, MN : Sparkhouse Family, 2017. |
Audience: Ages 3-5. | Audience: Pre-school.
Identifiers: LCCN 2017030302 | ISBN 9781506420776 (hardcover : alk. paper)
Subjects: LCSH: Bible stories, English.
Classification: LCC BS551.3 .B463 2017 | DDC 220.95/05--dc23 LC record
available at https://lccn.loc.gov/2017030302

VN0004589; 9781506420776; FEB2018
Sparkhouse Family
510 Marquette Avenue
Minneapolis, MN 55402
sparkhousefamily.org

SPARK
HOUSE
FAMILY
sparkhousefamily.org